THE MONEY MOVERS

THE MONEY MOVERS

What Banks Do—and Why

Don Colen

DAVID McKAY COMPANY, INC.
New York

All photos courtesy of the Federal Reserve Bank of New York and Citibank N.A.

Library of Congress Cataloging in Publication Data

Colen, Don
The money movers.

SUMMARY: Explains banking in simple text and illustrations.
1. Banks and banking–Juvenile literature.
[1. Banks and banking] I. Title.
HG1576.C64 332.1 77-4535
ISBN 0-679-20432-6

10 9 8 7 6 5 4 3 2 1

MANUFACTURED IN THE UNITED STATES OF AMERICA

For Benjamin

Contents

1 Through the Looking Glass 1

2 How Money Moves Around 9

3 Where Money Comes From 23

4 Where the Money Goes 33

5 You Can See the Road Ahead 44

Glossary 53

CHAPTER ONE
Through the Looking Glass

A bank is a two-way mirror.

In the bank, you see people putting money into the bank and people taking money out. They are there to cash checks, make deposits, withdraw money from saving accounts or checking accounts, buy travelers checks, put valuable papers in safe deposit boxes, borrow money, pay back loans or buy U. S. Saving Bonds.

Looking through the other side of the mirror, you can see what people are doing with money in the world outside the bank. Every day of the week, millions of people exchange money for things in stores; pay for services provided by plumbers or electricians or doctors or lawyers; buy lottery tickets or bus tokens; pay taxes, make down payments on houses, or do any of the thousands of things that people do with money. And all of this activity starts or stops at a bank somewhere in the United States or maybe even a foreign country, half way around the world.

All of this paying and receiving needs a lot of banks because that is the business of banks. They move money from a place where it is available to a place where it is needed. In the process, banks provide the services that are necessary to get the money where it's needed. They can't do this unless they earn a profit.

There are a lot of banks. In the United States, there are about 14,500 *commercial banks, which are* the kind that come to mind when anyone says the word "bank." But there are also *savings* banks *(thrifts), savings and loan associations* and *credit unions,* which people also call banks. They *are* banks in a sense because the "thrifts" perform many services that commercial banks perform. They are deeply involved in the financial network that serves people, businesses, and governments across the country and around the world.

Commercial banks are different from other "banks" because they both serve individuals and businesses—from the gas station on the corner to very large corporations such as General Electric and Du Pont. Commercial banks were the first kind of banks. They didn't have tellers and they didn't give toasters and calculators to new customers, because the first commercial banks were formed to help America achieve special goals.

IN THE BEGINNING

One hundred and sixty-three years after the Pilgrims landed at Plymouth Rock and only five years before George Washington became the first president of the United States, the Massachusetts Bank opened its doors in Boston. It is still in business, along with 15,000 other commercial banks. Today, about 600,000 people live in Boston; 163 years ago, the population numbered only 17,000. Boston was a crowded shipping center. Ships sailed out of the harbor bound for England and Europe as well as the Caribbean islands. Whether they were engaged in the famous "triangular" trade that exchanged manufactured goods for slaves and for rum, or whether they were simply exchanging lumber for English cotton goods, a way had to be found to bridge the money gap that trade created.

The Boston merchant who bought lumber from a farmer in Western Massachusetts had to have some way of getting money between the time he paid the lumberman in America and the time, months later, when he received money from his English customer. That is where the bank entered into the transaction. It loaned him the money, which meant, in effect, that the bank said, "Here, use this money for the next six months, on two conditions: One, you have to guarantee to pay it back. Two, you have to pay me a fee." That fee, of course, is *interest*—payment for the use of the money. The "guarantee" could have been a *lien* on his goods, which gave the banker the right to take possession of the goods if the merchant didn't repay the loan. Or the "guarantee" might have been a lien on other property that the merchant owned.

Many of those first banks were formed to serve particular trades: the Merchants Bank, The Seamen's Bank, The Lumberman's Bank. These banks learned very quickly that there wasn't enough activity in just one industry, so they made loans to all comers, always with the same conditions that banks use today: They will lend money to almost anyone for a fee (interest) as long as the borrower proves that he can pay it back. Today, there are other ways to provide that proof, as we shall see later.

At the time the first bank was started, Americans, as well as the many immigrants who were coming to the United States, were moving West in considerable numbers. They continued that pioneering movement toward the western frontier until the end of the 19th century. By then, pioneers had reached the Pacific Ocean, and the continental United States became what it is today. But as the pioneers moved westward during the 1800s, the pattern was always the same. People dropped off along the way to start towns, beginning with a general store, a saloon, a church, and a bank. The owner of the general store was often the banker until the bank grew large enough to expand into its own building. As the first banks had financed the colonial merchants by tiding them over for a fee, these banks also financed the growth of frontier towns. They helped until farmers could get their crops to market, miners could ship ore, or cattle growers could feed and sell their stocks.

KINDS OF MONEY

As the number of banks grew, problems arose, particularly about the money that people carried in their pockets. Coins were good, but paper money was better. It is much easier to carry a dollar bill in your pocket than it is to be loaded down with 100 pennies. There were two important questions, however: Who would print the money? How would people know it was good? Both questions were answered for Americans by their experience in the years between the Declaration of Independence and Washington's inauguration. Under the Articles of Confederation, which set the rules for the American government before the Constitution was written, the government printed paper money to pay its soldiers, to feed them, and to do all of the things that a government normally does.

Because the government was poor and because it had little wealth of its own (no one paid taxes), its paper money gradually became worthless. The phrase, "not worth a Continental" originated with that experience.

As we have noted, early banks and the growing number that were started in the early 1800s began to print their own money. These banknotes were backed by money in a particular bank and *collateral* (the rights against property that were pledged to pay off a loan). But suppose that the Bank of East Kansas had printed bank notes against the collateral of crops that were being grown. Suppose, too, that a Bank of East Kansas banknote was accepted by a traveler going to New York. By the time the traveler reached New York in about ten weeks, two things might have happened. Another New Yorker, to whom the traveler tried to give the note, might not have been sure the note was any good and would accept the Kansas banknote for only part of its printed value. Also, if crops in Kansas had failed, the collateral given to the bank would have been worthless. Loans would not have been paid off and the bank could have failed.

Both of these cases were repeated time and again. Finally, in 1863, Congress passed The National Banking Act. Under that law, banks could become *national banks.* The federal government printed national bank notes backed by silver, gold, and the credit of the United States. The national bank notes were exchanged for the individual banknotes in circulation. And even though the individual bank could still print money under the new law, less and less was printed because people preferred to have Uncle Sam's money.

After nearly seventy-five years, the United States

finally had its own money. Still, some banks didn't join the National Banking System, and they continued to operate under state charters. These banknotes circulated side by side with the official notes until they gradually disappeared, because no one trusted them.

By 1900, commercial banks had expanded all over the country and a few had branches in other countries. Except for the computers and machinery that are available today, they were doing essentially the same kind of banking business they do now—lending to individuals and businesses, and accepting *deposits.* In the process of growth all through the 19th century, the usual form of payment became *checks.* A check is nothing but a piece of paper on which someone, who has money in the bank, instructs that bank to pay someone else the amount that is written on the check. If an individual had a deposit in a commercial bank, he could write a check on those funds and use it to pay a debt.

Also by 1900, in New England, deposits were about seven times greater than the notes in circulation. This trend toward the use of check money continued. In Boston alone, just after World War I, about 60,000,000 checks a year were "cleared," which is the way banks swap checks among themselves. The process of check clearing today is an automated national system. One large bank in New York for example, clears more than two million checks each day.

THE NEW BANKS

Concentration on new methods and increasing

attention to different kinds of loans to different kinds of companies plus the invention of the *instalment loan* in the late twenties led commercial banks to neglect saving accounts. As often happens when a demand springs up, someone rushed in to fill it. At that time it was the mutual savings banks. First started in 1816, their real growth has spurted since the 1920s. They accepted savings deposits and made *mortgage loans,* a kind of loan that's used to finance the purchase of a house. They later provided some of the products and services formerly supplied only by the commercial banks. In the 1950s, savings and loan associations (S&L's), also an older type of savings bank, began a drive in California in the same way that the savings banks concentrated in the North Atlantic states. Like the mutuals, the S&L's concentrated on mortgage lending. Finally, in the 1930s, people working in factories began to form credit unions. At first these were non-profit local organizations that helped workers borrow money at cheaper interest rates so they could stay out of the hands of "loan sharks." Loan sharks make desperate borrowers pay back much more than they borrowed—or suffer the consequences. The resources of credit unions are now about a hundred times greater than they were just after World War II.

The different kinds of "banks" are beginning to lose their identities. That's why this is a good time to ask, "What *is* a bank?" The answer is far different from the one you would have gotten just a few years ago. The nature of banking is changing rapidly. Banks are at the entrance to a wide thruway and all the roads that reach back a hundred years are coming together to form a main artery into the future. The feeder roads are occupied separately by commercial banks, mutuals, S&L's, and credit unions. But on the thruway, you'll find only one kind of a bank. Even though they may keep their old names, they'll all be doing the same thing commercial banks do.

In the following pages we'll find out about commercial banks—what they do and how they do it. After that, we'll look ahead and follow that thruway into the future. But first, let's look at the service side of banking.

CHAPTER TWO

How Money Moves Around

You've never seen a Western in which John Wayne cashes a check in Cheyenne. It's not because checks weren't available during the lifetimes of the people he portrays in Westerns. As a matter of fact, by the Civil War, there was more check money in circulation than either coins or paper money. More likely, Big John simply felt better with a pocket full of change. Today some people call that change "walking-around-money" because the largest part of all the money in circulation–money that passes from hand to hand–is represented by checks. The reason for this development is convenience, which banks are improving every day.

A WORLD WITHOUT CHECKS

Money in circulation–coins and paper bills–won't disappear. It's too much trouble to write a check to pay for a newspaper and too time-consuming to write a check for a tankful of gasoline. But the amount of cash in circulation is getting smaller and smaller as the nation grows. Your parents * can tell you why.

* Both parents work in more than half the families in the U.S.

Let's consider your father's job and let's suppose that his take-home pay every month is $1,000,* only because that is an easy number to work with. And let's also suppose that the place where he works is a fifteen-minute drive to the north side of town and his bank is a fifteen-minute drive in the opposite direction. Two things could happen on pay day.

He could take the cash in his pay envelope to the bank as quickly as possible, holding out enough for your parents to pay for the things they buy during a week. Or, he could take the $1,000 home and parcel it out as your parents need it during the month and to pay bills at the end of the month. In the first case, someone would have to make a lot of trips to the bank. In the second case, too much cash would be lying around the house for a month. In either case, the nuisances would begin to add up, especially at the end of the month.

Most people have rent or mortgage, fuel oil, gas or electricity payments to make at the end of every month. In addition, many people have charge accounts at department stores (you buy things during the month and pay for them in one payment at the end of the month). If checks weren't available, your parents would have to make trips to the landlord's office or the bank that holds the mortgage on your house as well as the utility that sells electricity or gas to heat your house or the dealer who sells heating oil. They would also have to visit each store at which they had a charge account. Each trip would add to your parents' gasoline bill, if they drove, or increase

* Take-home pay is the amount of a person's pay after certain taxes have been deducted. These taxes are usually about one-fifth of the pay.

the amount they would have to pay for bus fares every month.

You can see that a world without checks could be a scary place with all that money lying around. It would be harder to keep track of how much money had been spent. It would also be a place where people wasted too much time. That's why checks were invented.

PAYING BY CHECK

Today, most people have checking accounts. Only one out of four families doesn't. They have to pay their bills in somewhat the way we described. Some of them make that chore easier by paying cash for *money orders,* which means that they are "buying" checks from companies that specialize in that service. For example, suppose your parents were in the group without checking accounts and they owed the Jones Fuel Oil Company $45 for last month's heating oil. They would take $45 in cash to the XYZ Money Order Company and give it $45 plus a service charge. The XYZ company would hand your parents a money order for $45, which your parents could mail to Jones. For people without checking accounts, money orders are useful, especially when it is a long distance from your home to the place where the bill has to be paid.

A check is the handiest way to manage money, for a check is nothing more than an order to pay.

Look at the picture of the check in this chapter. There is a place for the date, a line marked "pay to the order of," a line to write out the amount of money so that there can be no mistake about the amount of the check, and a place to sign the check. Always remember: you can't write a check if you haven't any money in the bank and it is against the law to write a check if you haven't got a checking account.*

When you write a check for $20 to Bill Smith, you are in effect saying to the bank, "Take $20 out of my account and pay it to Bill Smith." You then subtract $20 from the running total in your check book and the bank subtracts $20 from its records of your account. That's what your parents do when they pay their bills or write a check to pay for something they buy during the month. How checks get from person to person and back to the bank where they belong and eventually, at the end of the month, to the person who has the checking account, is the story of *check clearing.*

SIMPLE CHECKING

We saw what would happen if everyone used only cash. But now let's take another case. Instead of getting his pay in cash, or even in a check that he cashes, suppose your father takes advantage of his boss's offer to deposit his pay directly into his checking account in a local bank. What happens? If there's only one bank in town, "clearing" is pretty simple. Your father writes a check for $30 to the grocer, who deposits the check in his account at the bank. In this case, the bank *debits* (subtracts) your

* There are special accounts against which you can write a check when you haven't enough money in the bank because the bank has agreed in advance to lend you what you need to make the check good.

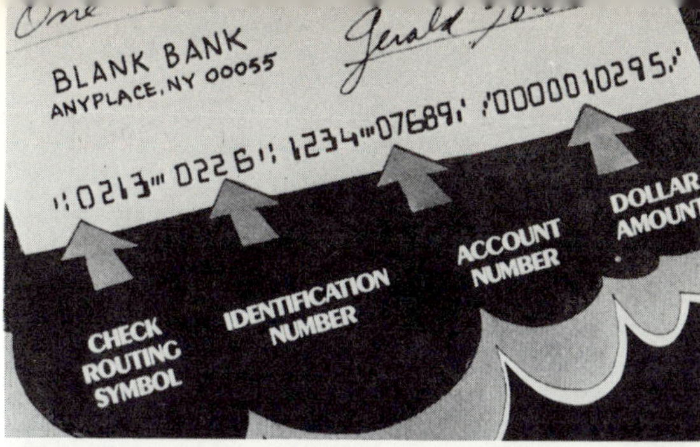

The magnetic numbers at the bottom of every check tell the computer what information to record.

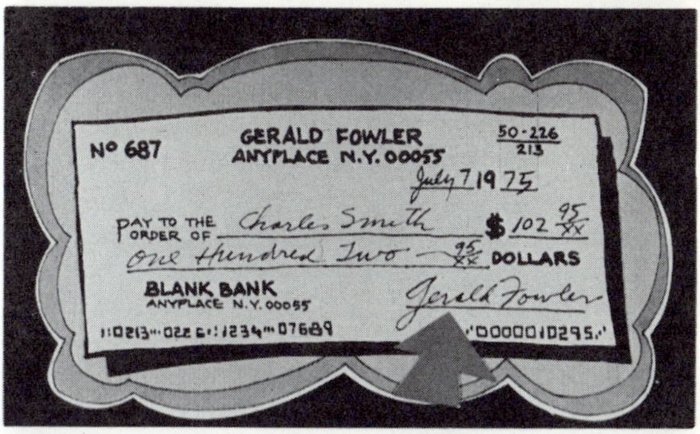

By signing this check, Mr. Fowler . . .

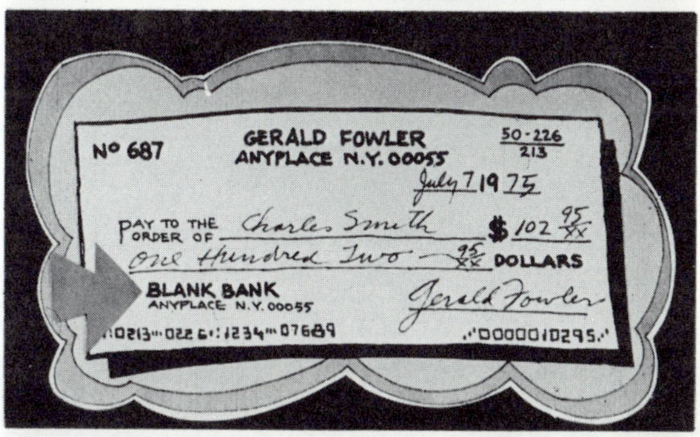

tells his bank . . .

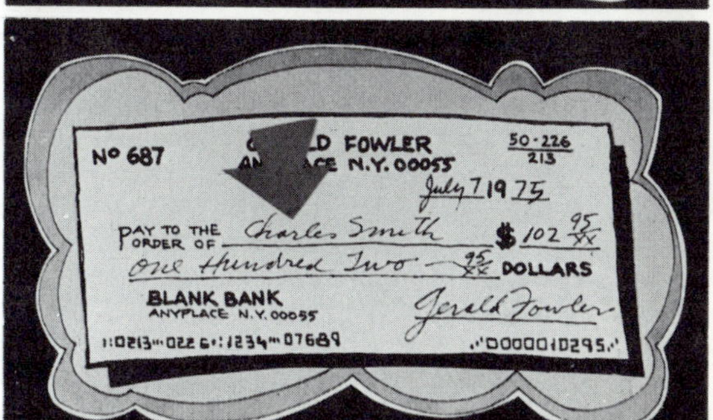

to pay Charles Smith . . .

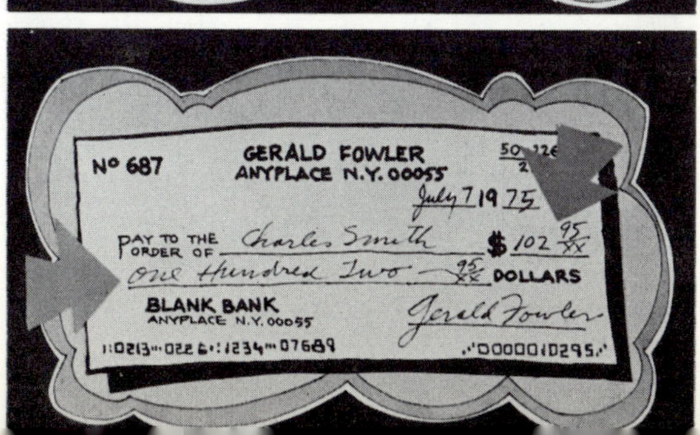

one-hundred and two dollars and ninety-five cents, and charges Mr. Fowler's account.

father's account for $30 and *credits* (adds) the grocer's account for $30. If there are two banks in your town, the system may take more steps. Your father might have his account in one bank and the grocer has his account in the other. Here's what happens:

Your father has written a check to the grocer who deposits the check in his bank. But there are a lot of other people who deposit checks in the grocer's bank, which they have gotten from people who have accounts in your father's bank. There are also many people with accounts in your father's bank who deposit checks that they have gotten from people who have accounts in the grocer's bank. The problem is to get the checks from one bank to another as simply as possible.

Every evening after the grocer's bank has closed for the day, it adds up the dollar amount of all the checks it has gotten from people who have accounts in your father's bank. At the same time, your father's bank adds up all the checks it has gotten from people who have accounts in the grocer's bank. Your father's bank then bundles up the checks it has gotten from people who have accounts in the grocer's bank and the grocer's bank does the same thing with checks from people who have accounts in your father's bank.

The banks exchange the bundles.

Maybe the total of all the checks drawn on your father's bank is greater than the total of all the checks drawn on the grocer's bank. Maybe it's just the opposite. Either way, at the end of every day one bank owes the other bank some money. To make things easier, they usually settle the differences once a week. This is the simplest kind of *check clearing*.

LONG DISTANCE CHECKING

Suppose, however, that you live in a large metropolitan area where there are several banks and each bank has a number of branches. Or suppose you live on the East Coast and your mother orders something from a store on the other coast. How would these checks be cleared? Exactly the same way they are cleared in a small one- or two-bank town. The process is not more complicated, but it does involve more steps—and the handling of an incredibly large number of checks. One bank in New York, for example, handles more than 2,000,000 checks every day of the week. Big banks may close their doors at three or five o'clock, but actually they work twenty-four hours a day. The way they can handle such enormous numbers of checks is to work through clearing houses.

CLEARING HOUSES

Take another look at the sample check. To the right of the date line, the large number 22 is that bank's branch number. The numerator in what looks like a fraction is the bank's identification number in a local clearing house. The denominator is a check routing number that indicates how the particular check is to be routed around the country.

Now look at the strange numbers at the bottom of the check. They are printed in magnetic ink so that they can be "read" by a computer. The first two blocks contain the same information that's printed in the "fraction" that we just talked about. It is those numbers that guide a check through the clearing system.

THE FEDERAL RESERVE SYSTEM

WHEN PRESIDENT WILSON SIGNED THE FEDERAL RESERVE ACT IN 1913, A NEW ERA BEGAN IN THE STORY OF CHECKS IN THE UNITED STATES.

THE ACT PROVIDES THAT EACH FEDERAL RESERVE BANK SERVE AS A CHECK CLEARING AND COLLECTION CENTER FOR THE BANKS IN ITS DISTRICT THAT HAVE ACCOUNTS WITH IT. THE SYSTEM PROVIDES A NATIONAL CLEARING MECHANISM THAT ELIMINATES THE LENGTHY REROUTING AND EXCHANGE CHARGES ON CHECKS. A MEMBER BANK THAT RECEIVES CHECKS PAYABLE OUT-OF-TOWN MAY NOW CLEAR THE CHECKS THROUGH ITS FEDERAL RESERVE BANK, BRANCH, OFFICE OPERATING A REGIONAL CHECK PROCESSING CENTER, OR CITY CORRESPONDENTS. CITY BANKS ENCOURAGE THEIR COUNTRY BANK "COUSINS" TO USE THEIR SPECIAL COLLECTION FACILITIES. THE CORRESPONDENT BANKING NETWORK AND THE FEDERAL RESERVE SYSTEM WORK HAND-IN-HAND TO PROCESS THE EVER-RISING VOLUME OF CHECKS THAT NEED TO BE COLLECTED.

DURING 1973 THE FEDERAL RESERVE SYSTEM HANDLED MORE THAN 9.9 BILLION CHECKS, AMOUNTING TO OVER 3.8 TRILLION DOLLARS. ALSO, OF COURSE, MANY OTHER CHECKS WERE COLLECTED BY CITY CORRESPONDENT BANKS, OR LOCAL CLEARING HOUSES, OR BY DIRECT PRESENTATION FROM ONE BANK TO ANOTHER.

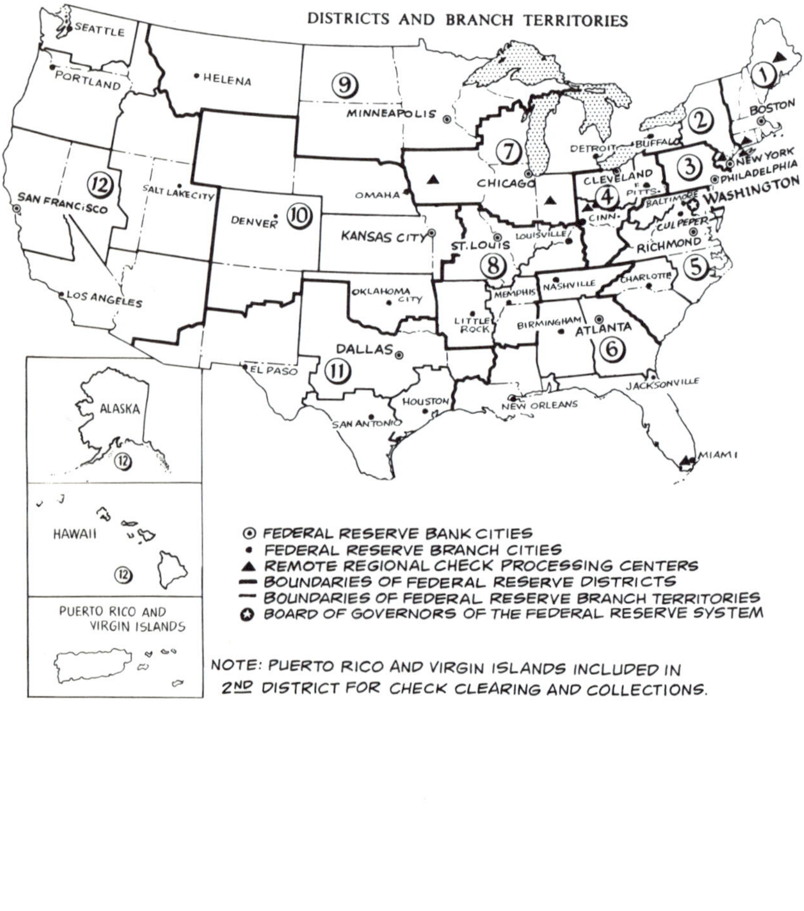

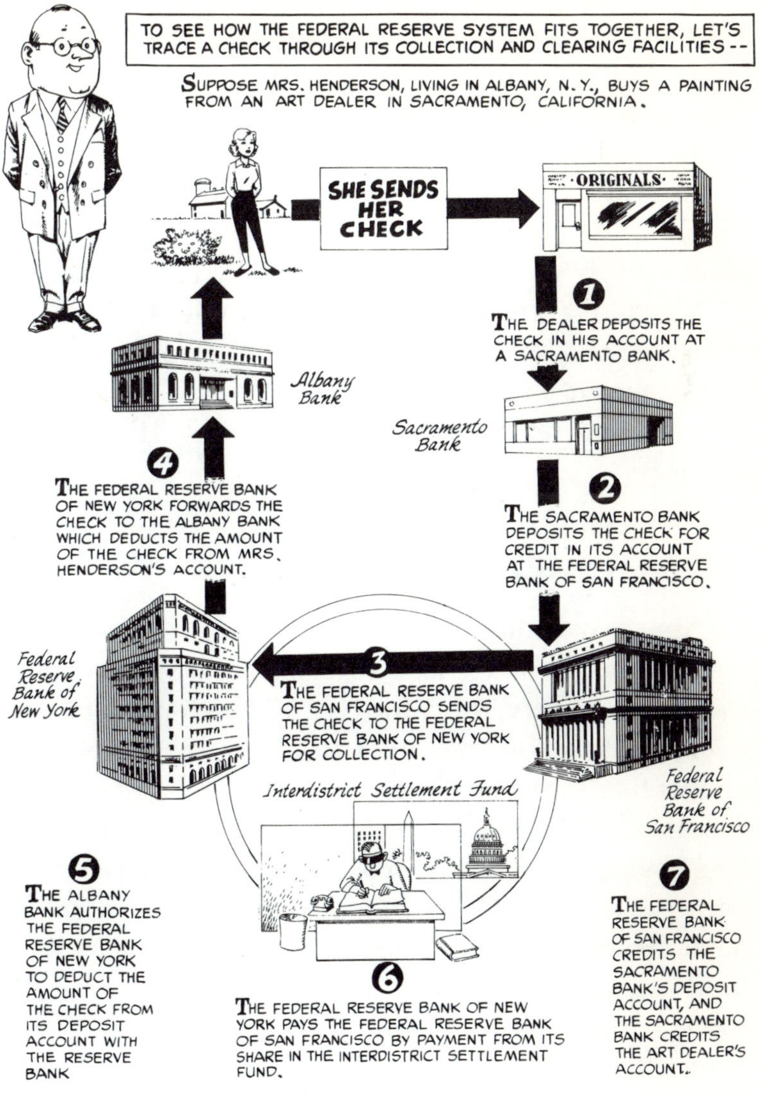
TO SEE HOW THE FEDERAL RESERVE SYSTEM FITS TOGETHER, LET'S TRACE A CHECK THROUGH ITS COLLECTION AND CLEARING FACILITIES --
SUPPOSE MRS. HENDERSON, LIVING IN ALBANY, N.Y., BUYS A PAINTING FROM AN ART DEALER IN SACRAMENTO, CALIFORNIA.
SHE SENDS HER CHECK
ORIGINALS
1 THE DEALER DEPOSITS THE CHECK IN HIS ACCOUNT AT A SACRAMENTO BANK.
Sacramento Bank
2 THE SACRAMENTO BANK DEPOSITS THE CHECK FOR CREDIT IN ITS ACCOUNT AT THE FEDERAL RESERVE BANK OF SAN FRANCISCO.
3 THE FEDERAL RESERVE BANK OF SAN FRANCISCO SENDS THE CHECK TO THE FEDERAL RESERVE BANK OF NEW YORK FOR COLLECTION.
Federal Reserve Bank of San Francisco
Federal Reserve Bank of New York
4 THE FEDERAL RESERVE BANK OF NEW YORK FORWARDS THE CHECK TO THE ALBANY BANK WHICH DEDUCTS THE AMOUNT OF THE CHECK FROM MRS. HENDERSON'S ACCOUNT.
Albany Bank
Interdistrict Settlement Fund
5 THE ALBANY BANK AUTHORIZES THE FEDERAL RESERVE BANK OF NEW YORK TO DEDUCT THE AMOUNT OF THE CHECK FROM ITS DEPOSIT ACCOUNT WITH THE RESERVE BANK
6 THE FEDERAL RESERVE BANK OF NEW YORK PAYS THE FEDERAL RESERVE BANK OF SAN FRANCISCO BY PAYMENT FROM ITS SHARE IN THE INTERDISTRICT SETTLEMENT FUND.
7 THE FEDERAL RESERVE BANK OF SAN FRANCISCO CREDITS THE SACRAMENTO BANK'S DEPOSIT ACCOUNT, AND THE SACRAMENTO BANK CREDITS THE ART DEALER'S ACCOUNT.

Big cities such as New York have their own clearing houses through which member banks do their own clearing within metropolitan areas. But essentially, clearing of checks across the country is done through the *Federal Reserve System,* or "the Fed" as it is popularly known.

The Fed is run by a board in Washington and consists of twelve district banks and their branches, which act as bankers' banks. They clear checks, lend money to banks, provide services to the country's private banks, and so forth. To clear checks, the Fed has devised a modern, high-speed electronic system that makes it possible for funds to "travel" across the country and return in less than a week. It happens this way:

A CHECK TAKES A TRIP

Suppose you live in Albany, New York and your mother has sent a check to a shop in Sacramento, California to pay for a sweater. The shop owner in Sacramento takes the check to his bank. The Sacramento bank deposits the check to its account with the district Federal Reserve Bank in San Francisco. The Fed in San Francisco credits the Sacramento bank's account with the amount and the Sacramento bank credits the seller's account in San Francisco.

At the same time, the San Francisco Bank sends the check to the New York Fed for collection. New York Fed pays San Francisco Fed and forwards the check to your mother's bank in Albany. It *debits* your Mother's account and the whole transaction has been completed. This national system operating through the twelve district banks of the Fed is now

The way checks used to be handled before the introduction of the computer.

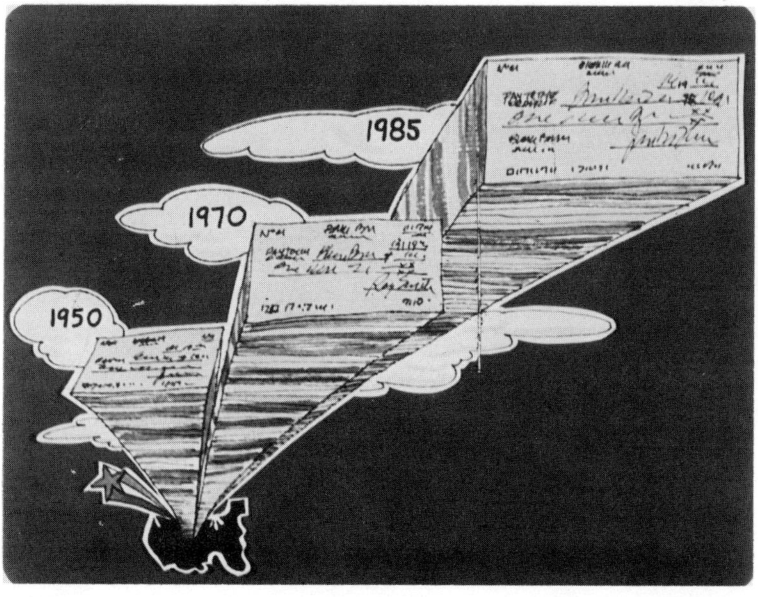

handling over thirty *billion* checks each year and is expected to have to handle double that amount in less than ten years, which is just about impossible. That is why many people in private banks and the Fed are working on an electronic system tied to computers so that all those checks won't have to be shipped all across the country.

COMPUTER TO COMPUTER

As you know, computers can store information on reels of tape that look like reels of movie film. One average eleven-inch reel, for example, can store all the information that's now contained in one million checks. Consequently, there is no reason why banks shouldn't be able to exchange reels of computer tape. Some local clearing houses are doing that now. Of course, the process is not quite as simple as we've described and a lot of questions will have to be answered before the system can go into effect. For example, most people want their checks back so that they can read them against the monthly statement that the banks send to checking-account depositors. There is also the question of needing a check to prove that payment has been made.

Finally, there is the important requirement for all kinds of expensive advanced equipment, such as automatic, high speed check-sorting and check-reading machines. But the day of automated check-clearing systems is coming. It must, or the country will choke on checks.

You may think from this trip through what is usually called "the payments mechanism" (which includes credit cards) that *paying* checks is all a bank

The control panel of the kind of automatic check sorting machine that enables some banks to sort as many as 2 million checks a day.

A stack of computer tapes ready for use.

does. You would be wrong. A check is only a way of getting into a system that is basically geared to *lending* money. But first, let's find out how money gets into the banks in the first place.

CHAPTER THREE
Where Money Comes From

The notorious bank robber, Willie Sutton, used to say that he robbed banks because "That's where the money is." The question that never bothered Willie was, How does the money get *into* the banks? And another question: Where does a bank get the money it needs to stay in the business of banking? To find the answers, let's imagine that we're going to start a bank. At the very beginning, remember one thing: Banks pay for every penny they get. That's the reason for interest rates, which are a measure of the cost of money, or saying it another way, interest rates are the price of money.

LONG, LONG AGO

Prices are set in *markets.* That is as true today as it was in ancient times. For example, 2,000 years before Christ was born, merchants from India, Egypt, and what is now Turkey, met to exchange their wares in Tyre, a city in Asia Minor. Maybe the price of a rug was fifty bushels of wheat or twenty-five bales of cotton. The price changed from day to day because it depended on the bargaining skill of the merchants, as well as supply and demand.

This same process took place wherever one person or a group of people had something that other people wanted.

At about the same time that merchants were meeting in Tyre, fishermen in the South Sea Islands were trading the fish they caught for the food that individual islanders grew in the fields around their huts. But here too, prices depended on haggling with very little assurance that fifty fish on Tuesday would exchange for the same four bags of potatoes that the fish had brought the day before. Sooner or later, someone had to find a better way, and sooner than later the better way turned out to be money.

FROM SHELLS TO PAPER

No one really knows when money was invented or who invented it. It was a simple but good idea then and it still is. Remember that the original notion was to find something which had a value that would be the same tomorrow as it is today. If money isn't worth as much tomorrow as it is today, someone is tinkering with it. That is as true today as it was when money was first used.

The first money wasn't the same as the money in your pocket. It was shells or beads or certain kinds of stones. When the first settlers came from Europe to America in the 1600s they found that the American Indians used strings of beads called wampum as their form of money. Over the years, beads and stones were replaced by precious metals such as silver and gold. But the basic idea was always the same. It was easier to say that 100 bushels of wheat cost one ounce of gold and 100 bales of cotton cost, say, one-half ounce of gold. It was easier for a merchant to sell the wheat, get the gold, and use it to buy cotton than it was to bargain over how many bushels of wheat would exchange for how many bales of cotton.

THE PRICE OF MONEY

Where did interest enter the picture? Originally, a scene something like this must have taken place. Marco, an Italian trader, met Wang, a Chinese trader, in the marketplace of Constantinople.

Marco: "Wang, old friend, I need your help. I want to buy a hundred camel hides, which cost eight pieces of gold. But I won't have the gold until Friday when I expect to sell fifty bottles of wine. Can you lend me eight pieces of gold until then?"

Wang: I would like to help you, Marco, but I need my gold to buy cotton today. Still, I will lend you the eight pieces today, if you'll give me back nine pieces on Friday."

Marco: "My friend, you are a thief."

Wang: "Not really. If I do not lend you the money today, I can buy my cotton. If I lend you the money, I must wait until Friday to buy my cotton. By then, most of the cotton may have been purchased and I will get only ninety bales for my gold. I am taking a risk, and even though we are old friends, I ought to be paid for the use of my money. That is why I ask you to give me an extra piece of gold."

EVERYBODY WINS

That is how interest came about. Marco was paying one extra piece of gold—the cost to him of borrowing money. Wang was receiving one extra piece of gold, which was the return on the money he loaned. Some merchants made enough money lending money that they stopped trading and became money lenders. The price they charged for lending money was the interest rate. They got their money by "renting" it from people who had it and lending it to people who needed it. They paid the people an interest rate for its use and they charged the borrower an interest rate for lending it. From the standpoint of the person who let the money lender use his money, the interest rate was *income.* From the standpoint of the person who borrowed from the money lender, the interest rate was a *cost.*

In order to make a profit the money lender charged the borrower more than the money lender had to pay for the use of the money. This is essentially how banks do business today, but the banking business is more complicated because larger sums are involved and there are many more ways that money can be used than when Marco and Wang invented interest. To understand what happens, let's start a bank.

WHO WATCHES THE BANKS?

You can't just start a bank for one very good reason: banks deal in other people's money. Every penny they handle belongs to someone else, which means that if the banker makes a mistake someone else pays for it. That is why there is insurance on saving accounts and so many regulations as to what bankers can and can't do. In the United States there are four major bodies that keep an eye on the banks. They are:

Each of the fifty states has a Superintendent of Banks. He tells banks operating in his state what they can and cannot do. He can also *charter* banks, which is essentially giving a group of people the right to start a bank—providing they pass certain character tests, prove they know something about banking, and have enough money to open a bank.

The Comptroller of the Currency watches over National Banks, which are banks that can be chartered under the National Banking Act of 1863. That Act was the first attempt by the Federal government to straighten out the country's banking system.

The Federal Deposit Insurance Corporation (FDIC) provides insurance up to $40,000 for each account. If a bank gets into trouble and goes out of business, depositors are protected. The FDIC also keeps an eye on banks to make certain that they do business in a way that will prevent them from getting into trouble.

Finally, the Federal Reserve System (Fed) is composed of all the banks that belong to the system and is known as the "bankers' bank." The Fed is America's *Central Bank*. Every country has one. The Fed, as we have seen, provides check clearing mechanisms, makes loans to banks when money is hard to come by *(tight money),* and generally watches over the country's money supply.

THE BIRTH OF A BANK

If we wanted to start a bank we would run into one or another of these four agencies. Each would ask much the same things: Who are you? What do you know about banking? How much money are you going to start with, which is what they mean when they ask: how much *capital* do you have? They are trying to make certain that the new bank will have enough money to carry on the business. Assuming you are an upstanding member of the community and know what you're doing, the big question is going to be "money" because the economy has grown to staggering proportions. One New York bank, for example, began in New York in 1812 with $800,000. Then the city had a population of 100,000. Today, the bank has a capital of $4 billion. New York has a population of 7.4 million people, and the bank does business all over the world. The original capital of that New York bank was put together by a dozen people, for that was too much money for one person to invest. Today most new banks begin with much more capital, which is accumulated by hundreds of people. They are the bank's stockholders. Since a crowd can't run anything, they vote for a Board of Directors, which in turn elects a Chairman. He hires the President and the bank is ready for business.

There is a catch, to be sure. The stockholders didn't invest their money in the bank because they love each other. They expect to earn money, more money than the usual rate of interest. Otherwise, the stockholders would have put their money in a savings account in another bank. They expect their *profit* will be somewhat higher than the savings bank rate. How much higher depends on the amount of profit they want to put back in the bank to increase its capital. That is how a bank grows. The more capital it has, the more loans it can make. The more loans that are made, the higher the profits it can earn.

THE DOORS OPEN

So let's open the door of our new bank. Some people come in to open checking accounts, and some put their money in savings accounts. The checking accounts are called *demand deposits.* A depositor can draw against it at any time, *on demand.* Most such deposits don't stay in the bank very long because people and companies keep as little money in the bank as possible. They want to use their money profitably. Still, in many instances, banks require their depositors to keep minimum balances, and whatever the total of all balances, the banks must keep a percentage reserve with the Federal Reserve Bank in its area. The same is true for *time deposits.*

So far, people have been putting money into our new bank. Now someone comes in for a loan. How much will we lend him? First, by law we can't lend anyone more than one-tenth of our capital. Secondly, we won't lend him any more than we think he can pay back. And thirdly, the amount we lend him will depend directly on the amount of money other people have deposited in our bank. That is really the business of banking. We take other people's money, pay them interest for its use, and make sure we can pay it back any time they want it.

A bank can generally lend out about five times what it has on its books from whatever source, plus what is due from other people. Very few banks fail over the span of a year, but those that do usually go out of business because the bankers were not careful about the loans they made. The chances are good that they have not kept up with the times.

For example, there used to be a charge for checking accounts, but the pressure of competition among banks has led to the "free" checking account, which more and more banks are offering. The amount of "other people's money" that banks have to lend has decreased over the years, and banks now regularly "buy" money to have more money to lend. They buy money in several different ways.

BOUGHT MONEY

Remembering that banks make on the average less than one penny of profit for every dollar they lend, fractions of a percent can make a lot of difference when you are dealing in hundreds of millions of dollars and thousands of accounts. In fact, bankers usually talk in terms of *basis points,* which are hundreths of one percent. A few basis points can make the difference between a profit and a loss. When a bank goes out to buy money, it wants to buy it as cheaply as possible.

One way they do this is to borrow each other's reserves overnight. Since a bank is making many, many loans every day of the week and the total of its deposits changes rapidly, some banks have more reserves on deposit with the Fed than they need. Other banks don't have enough, and those with a surplus lend to those whose reserves aren't up to the requirements of the reserve regulations. These funds are called *Fed Funds* and the interest rate is quoted on an annual basis. The actual overnight payment per one percent of interest is about a third of a basis point (100 basis points divided by 365 days). On a million dollar transaction with the Fed Fund's annual rate at, say, five percent, one bank will pay another bank somewhere around $140 for the use of the first bank's money.

Certificates of Deposit (CD's) are another method that banks use to buy funds. There is first the "small" CD for any sum from $25 to $100,000, and secondly, the "negotiable" CD, which can run into millions of dollars. Both are pieces of paper that state the fact that someone has "deposited" such-and-such an amount of money with the bank and the bank promises to repay the money, plus interest.

Except for these facts, the two kinds of CD's are different. The "negotiable" CD can run from 30 days to a year and longer. Whoever buys it can sell it to anyone else. They are usually bought by very big companies that have extra cash. For instance, an auto company might have extra cash from the sale of autos, and it won't need the cash until it has to buy more steel to make its new model cars. Rather than keep the cash in its checking account, where it doesn't earn any interest, the company buys a CD. In case the auto company needs cash sooner than it is expected, the company can take advantage of the "negotiable" feature and sell the CD.

The "small" CD is *not* negotiable and the buyer usually has to hold it for perhaps as long as four years. Because he agrees to hold it a long time, and not keep his money in a savings account, where it can be withdrawn quickly, the bank will pay a higher rate of interest on the CD than it pays on money in a savings account.

There are other ways that banks "buy" money, but Fed Funds and CD's account for the greater part. Money, in short, is the steel and rubber and copper and oil—the raw materials—of a bank. If you added up all the money in all the banks in the country, you would find that:

84 billion dollars is capital (the amount that stockholders put into the bank plus the profits that were kept in the bank).

298 billion dollars is in *time* deposits (savings accounts).

337 billion dollars is in *demand* deposits (checking accounts).

Your next question should be: what do banks *do* with all that money?

CHAPTER FOUR
Where the Money Goes

One of America's most outspoken Presidents, Harry S. Truman, said once that "a banker will only lend you money when you don't need it."

Of course, the President was only speaking for effect. During his years in office, the U. S. Government had borrowed billions of dollars, and most of it had come from the banks, for that is where money is borrowed.

Your parents may have borrowed from your local bank to get a *mortgage* on your house or to buy a car. Your uncle may have borrowed enough money to buy a boat. The local newspaper probably borrowed at one time or another to acquire a new printing press and the country's big auto-makers borrow to build new plants and equip them with machinery. Everybody borrows and a bank will lend to any person, any company, or any government as long as the bank is assured that the borrower can pay back the money in a reasonable length of time. "Reasonable" varies; it may mean overnight or thirty years.

WHAT IS A LOAN?

How often have you heard someone say, "Hey, can you let me have a quarter until Thursday?" That someone is really saying: "I need a quarter today,

Tuesday, and I haven't got it. Will you let me use your quarter from Tuesday until Thursday?"

If the lender believes his friend's story, he will lend the quarter. No matter what type or how big, that's all there is to a loan—with one exception. When a bank makes a loan, it charges interest for the length of time the loan lasts. Furthermore, when one friend lends another friend a quarter, he is going through all the factors that affect all kinds of loans.

There is the *amount* of the loan (the quarter), the *terms* of the loan (when it will be paid back and how), the borrower's *credit rating* (one's belief that a friend will pay back the loan based on previous experience with that friend), and the cost of the loan (the interest rate being charged). In this case, since the lender didn't ask his friend to return more than the friend borrowed, the cost of the loan was zero. When a bank makes a loan, there is a little more work involved than when one friend makes a loan to another.

EVERYBODY BORROWS

There are about 14,500 commercial banks in the United States. In 1976, all of those banks put together loaned 118 billion dollars to customers. Saying it another way, every year three out of four people in the United States borrow in one way or another from a bank. Basically, there are two types of loans to individuals: one is a *personal loan* and the other is a *secured loan.* A personal loan is an act of faith. In fact, most people are so honest that more than ninety-eight out of every hundred dollars loaned to individuals is returned. Most of the loss is due, not to dishonesty, but to the fact that the borrower had overextended himself. He borrowed more than he could possibly pay back or perhaps he lost his job.

These are events that one cannot always foresee. That is why banks ask so many questions when people come in to borrow. Of course, there's one other basic reason, which is that all the money that the banks hold belongs to someone else. Now let's see how borrowing works.

Suppose your family's old refrigerator has broken down. Your parents have been saving for a new one but the old one didn't last as long as they expected. Their savings don't quite match the price of a new refrigerator and they need another $300. They believe they will have that much in six months, so they go to the local bank to apply for a six-months' personal loan for $300.

The bank will want to know the amount of your parents' income. Maybe they both work, or maybe only one of them has a job. The questions make sense if you remember that the bank will lend to anyone who can reasonably prove that he or she can pay back the loan: Where do they work? How long have they held those jobs? Do they rent their home or apartment? Or do they own their own house? Do they have any other loans outstanding? Do they have *charge accounts?* These questions are asked only to learn whether your parents have other obligations that would make it difficult for them to take on the payments for a new loan.

CREDIT BUREAUS

Then, as a last check, the bank will ask a *credit*

TRW CREDIT DATA

JANE REYNOLDS
3 OAK STREET
Berkeley, La. 49027

20 JUST RD
FAIRFIELD NJ 07006
(201) 575-0720
(212) 964-3220

DATE OCTOBER 17, 1975

Dear Consumer:

In response to your recent request, we are providing this transcript of the credit information maintained by TRW Credit Data under the name and address(es) you have submitted.

IF you disagree with any of the information shown below:

Please PRINT your comments next to the item(s) in the "CONSUMER COMMENTS" column, then SIGN on the reverse side and return this form in the enclosed envelope. Additional information regarding these items may be supplied in the "ADDITIONAL COMMENTS" area on the reverse side.

NOTE: Please read the reverse side for additional "INSTRUCTIONS" and for "DEFINITIONS" of some of the terminology used below.
PAGE 1

	CONSUMER COMMENTS *(IF ANY)*
(POS) PAID SATISFACTORY ACCT REPORTED IN 5/75 BY FIRST NATIONAL CITY--UNSECURED LOAN--ORIGINAL AMOUNT $1300--FOR 12 MONTHS--ACCT OPENED IN 5/74--ACCT #177801038	
(POS) PAID SATISFACTORY ACCT REPORTED IN 5/74 BY FIRST NATIONAL CITY--UNSECURED LOAN--ORIGINAL AMOUNT $600--FOR 12 MONTHS--ACCT OPENED IN 4/74--ACCT #621604195	
(POS) OPEN TO CHARGE REPORTED IN 5/75 BY F N C B MST CHG--CREDIT CARD--CREDIT LIMIT $500--REVOLVING TERMS--ACCT OPENED IN 5/75--ACCT #90934514	
(POS) OPEN TO CHARGE REPORTED IN 10/74 BY BLOOMINGDALE BROTHERS--CHARGE ACCT--CREDIT LIMIT OR HIGHEST AMOUNT $500--TERMS/30 DAY CHARGE--ACCT OPENED IN 6/73--ACCT #10919686	
THANKS FOR THE OPPORTUNITY TO SERVE YOU	

A sample report of a customer's credit rating supplied by a leading credit bureau.

bureau for a report on whichever of your parents will be responsible for the loan. Credit bureaus are nationwide organizations that service stores and banks that regularly extend credit. Banks and stores report to them their experience with people who have charge accounts and who have borrowed from banks. In your father's case, for example, a credit report will state where and when he might have borrowed or charged before and whether he pays his bills on time. There is nothing secret about a credit report and anybody can get a copy of his own credit report from the credit bureau by paying a small fee. The same principle holds for credit bureaus that specialize in providing financial information about businesses. In both types of bureaus, the reason they exist is to make it easier for everyone. In your father's case, the bank can go directly to the credit bureau instead of writing to a number of stores and banks to verify your father's statements. And since handling and filing all those letters would cost money and time, the amount of interest the bank charges is less than it would be without the existence of the credit bureau.

THE NEVER-NEVER

All personal loans today are *instalment loans,* which are loans that are paid off over a period of time in equal "instalments." In England, when someone takes out a loan, they call it being "on the never-never." The reason is that in the early days of personal loans, some lenders were not honest and made it impossible for people to pay off the loan. Some of them were "never, never" paid off. Today, as we have seen, very nearly all loans are repaid.

The bank now has all the information it needs to extend that $300 loan. It has checked the statements your father made and the credit bureau says your father has a good *credit rating* (he pays his bills on time). The bank decides that your parents can handle the extra payments and gives them a check for the amount of the loan. Your father then signs a *note* promising to pay back the loan.

Of course, your father will also have to pay interest on the loan. Let's say the interest rate, in effect, amounts to 12 percent per year, which on $300 is $36 (300 times .12). But this loan is for only six months, bringing the actual interest charge down to $18. In this case, your father will have to pay back $318. Since most loans are repaid on a monthly basis, your father will have to pay the bank about $53.60 on the first of every month for six months. At the end of the sixth month, the loan has been repaid, together with the interest.

In the small number of cases where loans are not repaid, the bank has to go to court and sue the borrower to recover its money. The *collateral loan* was invented to avoid that kind of situation. Auto loans are collateral loans. The borrowing process is identical with the way your father got the loan for the new refrigerator. Information has to be provided and a credit check is made. But in the case of an auto loan, the borrower has to sign a note that gives the lender the right to take the car if the loan is not repaid.

If the loan isn't repaid the lender takes title to the car and sells it. If he gets enough from the sale to make up what's owed, the loan is cancelled. If the lender doesn't get enough, the difference between what he got from the sale of the car and the total amount of the loan is still owed by the borrower.

But no matter what the purpose of a particular loan, all of the loans that banks make to individuals fall into those two classes: personal *unsecured* loans; or *collateral* or secured loans. That holds true whether the loan is called a Boat Loan or a Home Improvement Loan or a Vacation Loan.

MORTGAGES

If your parents own your home, they have a

mortgage on it simply because few people have all the cash they need to pay for a house. Getting a mortgage is not very different from getting any other kind of a loan. A mortage is merely an instalment loan to buy a house. A mortgage loan is paid back over a much longer period of time, usually from 20 to 40 years. The *mortgage,* so-called, is an actual piece of paper on which all the conditions of the loan are written. The bank "holds" the mortgage until the mortgage loan has been paid.

To see what happens, let's suppose your parents are going to buy a house that costs $100, to use an easy figure. They have saved up $20, which can be used for the "down payment." This is the amount of their own money that they will use toward buying the house. A down payment is always required. That $20 is 20 percent of the price of the house, which is about average across the country. Down payments can range from 10 percent to as high as 50 percent. When people buy houses there are all kinds of technicalities that have to do with the land and the condition of the house. But, basically, in deciding to give a mortgage loan, the bank goes through the same process it does when it gives a personal loan. It asks the same questions and makes the same kind of a credit check. Then the bank figures out the monthly instalment.

In our case, your parents would be asking for a loan of $80 (cost of the house, $100, less the down-payment, $20) to be paid over 20 years. Dividing $80 by 20 results in a payment of $4 per year or 37 cents a month. In the same way, the interest on the loan for 20 years is calculated on a monthly basis and added to the 37 cents. The total is the amount your parents have to pay every month for 20 years. Although houses today actually cost many hundred times more than $100, the procedures and methods would be exactly the same. If your parents decided to sell the house in, say, ten years, they would have to pay off everything that was still owed on the mortgage loan from the proceeds of the sale.

BUILDING MORE FACTORIES

Businesses borrow money too. Let's consider the needs of an automobile manufacturer. He needs steel, paint, rubber, plastic, and many other things to build his cars. He has to pay for the raw materials and parts that go into a car before he sells the car and gets his money back. It is necessary for him to borrow money to carry him through that period. The company may need a new plant in which to build a new model car, but that plant won't be producing cars for a number of years. The company may borrow the money to build the plant. This was exactly what was done in building the Alaskan oil pipe line. The company that built the line borrowed money to buy materials and pay wages until the pipe line was finished and the builder got income from its use.

There are many ways that business loans can be written, but on the average they are instalment loans. The repayment periods may be in years rather than months. The company may have to put up collateral of one kind or another and the length of time required to pay back the loan may be a year or a period of years. Business loans are essentially instalment loans for very large sums of money, but these loans are not nearly as large as the loans that governments need.

RUNNING THE GOVERNMENT

Kings and emperors have always needed money. They needed money to pay for their living expenses and to pay their soldiers. And so they borrowed from the rich until their armies captured booty from their enemies. Then they could pay back the lenders. That was long before there were taxes.

Today, a government taxes its citizens to pay its expenses. It must borrow to keep going until taxes are paid. The sums governments borrow are enormous, so many governments "sell" *bonds.* Some bonds are simply promises to pay, such as U.S. Saving Bonds. People buy these bonds because they believe the promise of the United States Government. In fact, practically all the bonds sold by Uncle Sam, which run into billions of dollars each year, are sold as a promise to pay. States, cities, towns, schools, and water districts also raise the money they need by selling bonds. Often their credit or promises don't mean as much as Uncle Sam's, so often there are buildings or facilities backing the bond, like the house that backs your parents' mortgage loan.

Let's go back to your parents' mortgage loan. The amount of money your parents needed (the size of the mortgage) could be handled by one bank. In fact, some banks make as many as 50,000 mortgage loans every year. The loan that a government needs is often too big for one bank or even a group of banks to provide for any reasonable length of time, so the amount borrowed is cut up into pieces, which permits not only the banks but individuals to lend money to the government and earn interest.

For example, the Board of Education in your town

$75,000,000

STATE OF CALIFORNIA

SCHOOL BUILDING AID BONDS, SERIES AJ

($5,000 DENOMINATIONS)

New Issue. Dated September 1, 1976. Due September 1, 1977-96, inclusive.
Interest payable March 1 and September 1.

INTEREST EXEMPT FROM FEDERAL INCOME TAXES
UNDER EXISTING STATUTES AND DECISIONS

This announcement is not an offer to sell or a solicitation of an offer to buy the Bonds. A copy of the Official Statement describing the Bonds may be obtained in any state from such of the undersigned or other persons as may lawfully offer the Bonds in such state. The Bonds are offered, subject to prior sale, for delivery when, as and if issued and received by us and subject to approval of legality by the Attorney General of the State of California and Messrs. Orrick, Herrington, Rowley & Sutcliffe, Attorneys, San Francisco, California.

AMOUNTS, MATURITIES,
COUPONS AND
YIELDS OR PRICE

$3,750,000
DUE EACH SEPTEMBER 1

1977	4.60%	3.00%
1978	4¾	3.25
1979	4¾	3.50
1980	4¾	3.75
1981	4¾	4.00
1982	4¾	4.15
1983	4¾	4.30
1984	4¾	4.45
1985	4.80	4.60
1986	4.80	4.70
1987	4.80	100
1988	4.90	100
1989	5	100
1990	5	5.10
1991	5	5.20
1992	5¼	100
1993	5¼	5.30
1994	5¼	5.40
1995	5¼	5.45
1996	5¼	5.50

(Accrued interest to be added)

Redeemable beginning September 1, 1991 as set forth in the Official Statement.

CITIBANK, N.A.

MORGAN GUARANTY TRUST COMPANY
OF NEW YORK

UNITED CALIFORNIA BANK

SALOMON BROTHERS

CROCKER NATIONAL BANK

FIRST PENNCO SECURITIES INC. NORTH CAROLINA NATIONAL BANK

LANGDON P. COOK & CO. INCORPORATED LOEWI & CO. INCORPORATED THE ATLANTIC NATIONAL BANK OF JACKSONVILLE

C. S. McKEE & COMPANY INCORPORATED FIRST NATIONAL BANK OF MINNEAPOLIS

August 25, 1976

An advertisement for a typical loan to a government body showing the banks that are lending the money and the amount of interest on that loan.

plans to build a new school, which will cost a million dollars. Until tax money comes in, it will have to borrow the money. Here too, the same kind of credit appraisal is made. The bank lends the money to the Board, usually for twenty or thirty years. It then divides the loan into $1,000 parts or bonds. In most instances the bank cannot afford to make the loan by itself, so it sells all or most of the bonds to others. This kind of a loan does not normally require instalment payments. The school board pays the interest every three or six months to the holders of the bonds and *redeems,* or pays off the principal at the end of the loan, when they come due.

That is where the money goes: to people, to businesses, and to governments. The details of loans, the amounts, the time and the way the loan is prepared may differ from borrower to borrower. But essentially, all loans follow the same principle: the bank will lend money to anyone who can pay it back.

CHAPTER FIVE
You Can See the Road Ahead

Suppose that next to your telephone at home there is a screen that looks like a television screen and in front of it is a keyboard. By punching the right buttons, your parents could get a look at their checking account statement as of that moment. The same would be true for their savings account. Pressing other buttons, they could move money from their checking account to their savings account and back again, direct the bank to pay store bills and subtract the amount of the bill from either their checking account or their savings account, get a loan, make a payment on the loan, find out how much they still owed, and much more.

Impossible? Not at all. Most of it can be done right now and some is already happening. When will it all happen? Perhaps not in our lifetimes, because there are advantages to checks that electronics will never replace. But many of the functions and parts will be available in all banks, not just commercial banks, which is the kind of bank we've been talking about because all banks are becoming alike. Here is what's happening.

THEY'RE ALL THE SAME

In one place or another and in one part of the country or another all of the different kinds of banks are beginning to do the same kind of business. The first breach in the wall that separated commercial banks from savings banks was the so-called *NOW* (Negotiable Orders of Withdrawal) account. This was invented by a savings bank a few years ago in Massachusetts and is spreading across the country. What this device did was to make a savings account into a checking account. If your parents had a savings account in a savings bank, they got a book of Negotiable Orders of Withdrawal which looked just like checks and could be used as checks. These NOW "checks" cleared just like the checks of commercial banks and were accepted by everyone as checks.

The NOW account made it attractive to take checking accounts out of commercial banks and open NOW accounts in savings banks. The reason is that with the NOW account, savings banks were in effect paying interest on checking accounts, which is prohibited for commercial accounts. As a result, pressure is growing to scrap the prohibition against paying interest on checking accounts. Then all kinds of banks would be offering both checking accounts and savings accounts. Commercial banks are striking back with new kinds of machines.

YOU ARE THE BANKER

What's happening is that with little plastic cards that look like credit cards, cash machines, electronic devices, and computers, banks are letting people do a lot of their own banking. They don't have to stand in long lines waiting for busy tellers to handle hundreds of people. Customers can now do for themselves a lot

By using a special card, a customer can withdraw cash from the bank's machine 24 hours a day.

of the work that tellers used to do. Cash machines were the first step.

In many banks customers are now given *debit cards.* They look like credit cards, but they're not credit cards. They are information cards. Some have a black, magnetic stripe on the back (take a look at some of your parents' credit cards). That is where information such as a checking account number, the limits on the account and so forth is recorded. Other cards don't have a stripe, but use other means to store the necessary figures. These cards are the key to using the new machines.

For example, banks across the country are beginning to install cash machines. The customer dips his debit card into the machine, presses buttons to tell the machine how much cash he wants, and out comes the money. Of course, the money isn't free. The cash machine is hooked up to computers that keep all the bank's records. When the customer pushes buttons to tell the machine how much cash he wants, he is also telling the computer to deduct that amount of cash from the balance in his account.

Other banks are beginning to equip their tellers with computer terminals—devices no bigger than a shoe box. The terminal has a place to insert a debit card, a little window to show information, and a series of buttons. If the customer wants to cash a check someone has given him or his own check, he hands the teller his debit card. The teller inserts the card into the terminal and punches the amount of the check on the buttons. Within seconds, a message on the terminal window tells the teller whether the customer has enough cash in his account. If the customer wants to know how much money he has in his checking account, the teller can also find out from the terminal system.

One commercial bank in New York City has put these terminals out in the middle of the bank lobby so a customer can get his balance all by himself. The same bank is in the process of connecting the terminals and its computers so that a customer can move money from a checking account to a savings account and back again. Suppose a customer has $100 in his savings account and $50 in his checking account. He wants to write a check for $75, but he is $25 short. With the new system he simply inserts his debit card into the terminal on the lobby floor and pushes the right buttons to tell the computer to take

A terminal in a lobby of a bank that lets a customer check his own balance.

The same kind of terminal enables a teller to get similiar information on accounts.

$25 out of his savings account and move it into his checking account. Obviously, the average customer will keep as little money as possible in his checking account, where it doesn't earn interest. The computer terminal is the commercial banks' "secret weapon" against the savings banks' NOW account. That is also why the law against paying interest on checking accounts is likely to be repealed.

BANKS IN STORES

No one is really putting banks in stores, but banks are putting terminals in stores. If a customer in a store wants to cash a check or pay for something with a check, the same thing that happens at the bank's lobby terminal happens right in the store. The cashier in the store inserts the customer's debit card into the machine and punches the amount of the check. Within seconds, a message appears in the terminal window, telling the store owner whether the customer has enough money in the bank to cash the check or to use it as payment.

Not only are these terminals already in all kinds of stores, but the real action is in supermarkets. Believe it or not, more checks are cashed in supermarkets than in all the banks in the country. That's because your mother finds it a lot easier to bypass the bank and go directly to the market, where she can cash a check to pay for whatever she bought and have some money left over for the week's expenses. With the terminal, the cashier at the checkout counter can tell immediately whether the check is good. Your mother no longer has to see the store manager to get her check approved and the store manager doesn't have to spend time approving checks.

Where will this end? Nobody knows. So far, terminals in stores are used primarily for verification. But all the parts are in place to make it possible for your mother not only to cash a check at the supermarket, but to make a deposit as well. After all, the same computer serves all of the bank's functions. If the terminal can check the amount in your mother's account, there is no reason why she couldn't give the supermarket an additional sum of money. She could tell the clerk at the checkout counter to punch the terminal and credit the amount to your mother's account. This hasn't happened because taking a deposit means that the supermarket becomes a branch of the bank. So far, that has not been allowed.

AROUND THE WORLD

Every country, large or small, has at least one bank; many of them have thousands. Everything we've said so far applies not only to banks in this country but to banks all around the world. Of course, there are differences from country to country.

Some countries don't have savings and loan associations. There is nothing like a credit union anywhere else in the world. Most of the western countries have savings banks. But the differences from country to country are striking. For example, the United States is the only country that doesn't allow a bank in one part of the country to have a branch in another part. A bank here can only have branches within its own state, and in some states, a bank can't have *any* branches.

In England a depositor can write *overdrafts* on his

checking account, which means that, within reason, he can write a check when he hasn't any money in the bank. As you might expect, he must pay back the overdraft within a reasonable period of time. Each country has its own type of banks, its own laws, and its own kind of money, but nowhere in the world are people permitted to carry large sums of money from country to country. From what you've learned about how checks are exchanged among banks and cleared, you can see how money is moved by the money movers.

IT'S ALL IN THE SYSTEM

There are only two things you can do with money. You can save it—or you can use it. There are no other choices. If you hide it, you won't get interest on it and you can't buy anything with it. If you use it, you can buy something with it or you can invest it; that is, you can put it in a savings account, or buy a Government Savings bond or some other kind of security that pays a return like interest. But however you use it, the money ends up in a bank and travels from one account to another.

Let's say your father buys a U.S. Government Savings Bond. He gives a check to the bank to pay for the bond. The bank, to help out Uncle Sam, is serving like a store to sell the bonds. The bank gives your father the bond and sends the check to the Federal Reserve bank in your area. The Fed adds the amount of the check to the government's account. Then the government uses the money to pay its bills by writing checks for things it has bought. And so the money goes around and around, always staying within the banking system. The same thing happens from country to country. The figures showing who owes what to whom in individual banks change constantly, but the total money in the banking system around the world remains much the same.

BANKING IS A BUSINESS

That is the business and the value of banks. They move money from where it's available to where it is needed, and they charge for the service, which is the interest rate. In short, if you want a simple definition of a bank, call it a money shop.

And if you want a simple definition of a banker, call him the money mover.

Glossary

BONDS–Shares of a very big loan that are sold to individuals. Each bond pays the owner a fixed rate of interest, and the bond states the amount that is owed and when the bond will be repaid. The term of a bond may run from five years to as many as 30 or 40 years.

CHARGE ACCOUNT–A right that a store gives to a customer to "buy" things and pay later, usually at the end of the month.

CHARTER–A government's agreement for a group of people to start an organization, such as a bank or a corporation.

CHECK–An "order form" that tells a bank to move deposits from one account to another, or from an account in one bank to an account in another bank.

CHECKS, TRAVELERS–"Checks" for specific amounts, for example, \$10 or \$20 that can be bought and eventually used to pay bills. The two most popular travelers checks, First National City and American Express, are accepted all over the world.

CLEARING–The process of exchanging checks among banks so that money is moved from the account of the person who wrote the check to the account of the person to whom the check was written, regardless of where the people live or what banks are involved.

COLLATERAL—Property that is put up as a pledge that a loan will be paid back. If the loan is not repaid, the lender can take the collateral.

CREDIT—From a bank customer's point of view, an addition to his account. The opposite of *debit.*

CREDIT BUREAU—An organization that specializes in collecting information about people's payment habits. The information is made available to lenders.

CREDIT CARD—A plastic card that can be used to charge purchases in stores or restaurants as well as pay for hotel accommodations and transportation.

CREDIT RATING—The way lenders judge your ability to repay loans or pay off charge accounts.

DEBIT CARDS—A plastic card like a *credit card* that allows a depositor to take money out of his account with a bank, or transfer it.

DEBITS—From a bank customer's point of view, a deduction from his account. The opposite of a *credit.*

DEMAND DEPOSITS—Usually checking accounts.

DEPOSITS—Money that you have put into an account in a bank. Also used as a verb, describing the act of putting money into the bank.

FEDERAL RESERVE SYSTEM—America's central bank, to which any bank can belong. Also known as the "banker's bank."

INSTALMENT LOAN—A loan that can be paid back bit by bit, usually over the period of the loan. A five-year loan, for example, would be paid back in 60 equal "instalments" (5 years × 12 months). Each monthly instalment also includes interest on the loan.

INTEREST—From a bank's point of view, interest is

the amount the bank pays you, and is a cost to the bank for the use of your money. From your point of view, interest is the income you get on your money when you put it into a savings account. Interest is also the amount you have to pay for having the bank lend you money.

INTEREST RATE–The percentage of a loan or deposit that is used to figure the amount of interest you owe the bank or the bank owes you.

LIEN–A claim on property that has been put up as *collateral* for a loan that has not been paid back.

MARKET–A "place" where goods and services are bought and sold, such as the stock market or a local "flea" market. A market does not have to be in one place but may consist of a group of widely separated people who buy and sell certain things. For example, the "market" for postage stamps that some people collect is composed of all the stamp dealers across the country who keep in touch with each other and set the prices for stamps.

MONEY ORDER–A *check* that can be bought from a bank or a company that specializes in selling such checks. Money orders can be used to make payments.

MORTGAGE–A loan for the purpose of buying real estate. The mortgage is a written statement describing the property and the amount and terms of the loan.

NATIONAL BANK–Banks created under the National Banking Act of 1863 and regulated by the Comptroller of the Currency in Washington, D.C.

NOW ACCOUNTS–(Negotiable Orders of Withdrawal) Savings accounts on which a withdrawal slip can be used as a *check*.

PROFIT—The addition over what it costs to buy something that is received when the goods or services are sold.

REDEEM—Pay off bonds

SECURED LOAN—A loan for which some kind of *collateral* is pledged until the loan is repaid.

TERM—The length of time for which a loan is made.

TERMS—The conditions under which a loan is made, stating when the loan will be paid back and how.

TIGHT MONEY—A condition, usually during times of good business, when the demand for loans is very great and interest rates are high.

TIME DEPOSITS—Usually savings accounts.

UNSECURED LOAN—A loan made purely on the basis of your credit rating, which is the proof that you can repay a loan.